The Subjugation Of The Body

Hiram Erastus Butler

Kessinger Publishing's Rare Reprints

Thousands of Scarce and Hard-to-Find Books on These and other Subjects!

- Americana
- Ancient Mysteries
- Animals
- Anthropology
- Architecture
- Arts
- Astrology
- Bibliographies
- Biographies & Memoirs
- Body, Mind & Spirit
- Business & Investing
- Children & Young Adult
- Collectibles
- Comparative Religions
- Crafts & Hobbies
- Earth Sciences
- Education
- Ephemera
- Fiction
- Folklore
- Geography
- Health & Diet
- History
- Hobbies & Leisure
- Humor
- Illustrated Books
- Language & Culture
- Law
- Life Sciences
- Literature
- Medicine & Pharmacy
- Metaphysical
- Music
- Mystery & Crime
- Mythology
- Natural History
- Outdoor & Nature
- Philosophy
- Poetry
- Political Science
- Science
- Psychiatry & Psychology
- Reference
- Religion & Spiritualism
- Rhetoric
- Sacred Books
- Science Fiction
- Science & Technology
- Self-Help
- Social Sciences
- Symbolism
- Theatre & Drama
- Theology
- Travel & Explorations
- War & Military
- Women
- Yoga
- *Plus Much More!*

We kindly invite you to view our catalog list at:
http://www.kessinger.net

THIS ARTICLE WAS EXTRACTED FROM THE BOOK:

Narrow Way of Attainment

BY THIS AUTHOR:

Hiram Erastus Butler

ISBN 0766104583

READ MORE ABOUT THE BOOK AT OUR WEB SITE:

http://www.kessinger.net

OR ORDER THE COMPLETE
BOOK FROM YOUR FAVORITE STORE

ISBN 0766104583

Because this article has been extracted from a parent book, it may have non-pertinent text at the beginning or end of it.

Any blank pages following the article are necessary for our book production requirements. The article herein is complete.

The Subjugation of the Body.

THIRD LECTURE.

We will read to you a poem by one who for many years has been in isolation, devoting his thought and soul's aspiration toward Divinity, to know the mind of God concerning the sons of men.

"Now is the Cycle of the world complete,
And I, Humanity, once more behold
My spiritual Eden at my feet.
My fraudful foes are banished from my fold,
Melted like snow-flakes, vanishing away.
The Spiritual Heaven is bright with day;
Into my Heaven I've gathered from below
Myriads uncounted. Now shall Earth's last woe
Vanish. The Spiritual World being free,
Evil shall perish from earth utterly.
Wake, blinded World, from out thy ashes start—
From out thy dust arise thou mighty Heart,
Thrill with sweet joy. Humanity was one,
And shall be one again. Our Central Sun,
God Manifest, shall re-unite mankind.
All sons of men shall share one common mind,
Inspired, pervaded by Divinity.
O Earth, sweet child of God, thou'lt shine on high,
Wearing thy coronal of loveliest sheen,
Gemmed with all stars. Soon like a goddess-queen.

Amid a Paradise of nations free,
Thou'lt nurse at thy sweet breasts incarnate Liberty.

O Earth, sad Earth, how desolate thou wert,
With life-blood ebbing from thy fatal hurt;
With all thy mourning Nations bound in chains,
And smiling Plenty driven from thy plains;
With Vice and Want and Ignorance and Crime
Dethroning Art, Song, Beauty, Truth divine;
With festering Vices in thy fated breast,
And War's accursed heel trampling thy snowy vest.

O Earth, sweet Earth, thou, like a maniac child,
Wanderest through sorrow's wilderness; the wild,
Fierce storm hath wet thy garments, and thy head,
Crowned once with light, is death-like, garlanded
With wreathed contagions, serpents fierce and dire;
Thou standest 'mid thine own funereal pyre,
Consuming to white ashes. Thou shalt rise,
Reanimate, and thine shall be the prize
Of joy and victory. In Heaven again
The dust that now obscures the minds of men,
Quickened by spirit-fire, transformed, shall glow
Like crystal moon-beams shining on pure snow.
Matter, refined and purified, shall be
The floating garment of the Deity.
O glorious shall that New Humanity,
Gathered from scattered nations far and vast,
Build the wide Temple, where the mighty Past
And the great Future, like the Cherubim
Above the Mercy Seat, shall dwell within,
And the bright Present, where their pinions meet
Receive the Deity, whose utterance sweet,
Mankind inspiring, then and evermore
Shall echo to the skies; while every shore

By man inhabited with life shall bloom,
And earth no more have slave, king, dungeon-vault or tomb."

This seems to be a prophecy looking forward to a golden time when sorrow, want, pain, sickness, and death shall have passed away, when immortality shall be depicted on every face.

The question seems to be asked and echoed through our land and city: What is this Society Esoteric? What are its objects? What does it mean? It means simply this that we intend to unite all our forces, mental and spiritual, into one definite ultimate, viz.: bringing man up to a higher and grander sphere of existence. To do so we find it becomes necessary to begin with the basic principles of our own physical nature; first, learning the laws of life, the laws that govern our own physical body and its relations to the mental sphere; second, the laws governing the unfoldment of the mind to its highest ultimate, and uniting it to the spiritual and cause-world. In that grand ultimate, when the human mind shall find complete harmony between itself and the spiritual world, then the mind of Divinity will have its perfect expression in the mind of the individual. But for this we must begin with the understanding, carefully following the laws governing the unfoldment and development of our own physical body. We must first, in order to have a healthy mind, have a healthy, harmonious body. The body is not only the house we live in, but it is (in the symbolic language of the Bible), the horse we ride on, it is the instrument that allies us to the physical world and to all the uses relative thereto. Therefore it becomes necessary to put it in order, to have every part and particle of it working together in perfect healthful harmony. To do so in this world of chaos, in this age of distortion, we have a tast on hand, a task more difficult than it was some years ago. It does seem, and we think all will bear us out, that at the present time there is an almost insane appetite for sensual pleasure and gratification. It is surprising, of a Saturday night or a holiday or at any time when the masses of men are at liberty and on the streets, to find so many reeling under the influence of intoxicating liquors. I took a walk last evening, about three squares from the house, for rest, not thinking about the influence that I was going into and therefore not trying to protect myself. I found on my return home that my brain reeled as much as if I had drunk a large amount of liquor. It brought to my mind the words of the prophet **Jer.** where he says; "Drink ye, and be drunken, and   spew, and fall and rise no more."

It seems that there is a drunkenness in the very atmosphere. The earth is corrupted under its influence, society distorted, the world in chaos, worse probably than at any other period of the earth's history. Under these conditions for those who are the most fully and perfectly unfolded and, therefore, most sensitive and most affected by the psychic influences of such minds, — to bring into healthy and harmonious action this body of ours is a task, and a hard one. To do this, necessitates care in our food, that we feed the body properly, and see to it that all the processes of digestion should be in good working order, give the body nothing but that which will nourish it; and as we begin thus to care for our body, we shall find that it reacts upon the mind and will create like tendencies in the mental faculties. As we discriminate between the different articles of food we discover that it affects us favorably in discriminating between the different kinds of thought. Thus we perceive that, as soon as the mind begins to take hold of the body, it will organize itself into proper alliance with the laws and methods of nature. We cannot act upon our physical body without its reacting upon our mind. The more carefully we observe these laws, the more successful will our efforts to understand the great laws of the universe become.

In the most ancient writings from the Semitic side we find the name YAHVEH given as the name of God, the great mystic name to which we have called your attention so frequently before, because it is a centre around which all causation gathers and from which it emanates. It stands for the controller of all things, as is expressed in the words I WILL BE WHAT I WILL TO BE, this being the expression of Divinity in its highest attributes that man can conceive of. Man, if wise, will bend all his efforts toward becoming like that Divinity. We find that the man or the woman that is best capable of willing and doing according to their own good pleasure is the strongest, most successful, and the best citizen, and it is also the man or the woman that is capable of making the highest attainments in all departments of life.

We can have no adequate idea of the influence of the thought of government and control of our body, in its relation to appetites, until it is experimented on. As soon as you begin to think concerning what is proper for the body, and what is improper for it, begin to analyze the qualities of the food taken, and to make positive decisions to take nothing but what is absolutely necessary, and as you sit down to the table and discriminate between what you are going to choose, and what reject, you will find that you must reject the greater portion. As you do this you relieve the system from a great amount of burdensome or poisonous qualities that are constantly being used. If you were addicted to some habits that were beyond your power to control, or at least you thought them to be, no matter of what nature those habits were, you sit down to the table and begin to reason: "I am in the habit of taking strong coffee, it does not nourish my body, it does not feed, I can do without that,"—then decide positively "I will not use it." Again, here is pepper and other spices; of what use are they? None at all. Then the decision is made "I will not use them." Then go on, step by step, trying to find what food is proper for you. You will find that, no matter what habits you have had to overcome, they will be cast off in a very short time.

You will begin to see that the habit of controlling the body begins to promote within you a pleasure in that control, a consciousness of power that you never before possessed, a consciousness of the ability to be, and do, according to your own pleasure. Now, the world thinks that they are seeking pleasure when they are following the appetites and passions of their own physical body. In every effort that is made in that direction to obtain pleasure the direct opposite results. We have a land filled with the moans and cries of the sick and a diseased and poverty-stricken people, for no other reason than that there is no care for the government of the appetites and passions. To control the appetites and passions, ask yourself the question, "What is the use in this appetite?" Everything has its use. What was the original purpose in this appetite? Simply to teach you to discriminate between such articles of food as should be taken by you, and such articles as should be rejected.

We know that unnatural appetites may be created. In order to find out what in our appetite is normal, and what abnormal, we have got to bring ourselves down to the simplest and purest elements of food. I have brought myself down to live entirely on vegetable food, excluding rigidly everything else but the articles of food that were of pure vegetable production, not allowing myself to touch anything that had the elements of animal life in it. After following that course for a time, I began to find out what my real normal appetite was. It was thus demonstrated to me, how many tastes I had cultivated and created in myself. After that time, any of those unwholesome articles if I attempted to indulge in them were repulsive to me. When the appetite is brought down to pure nature, then we can begin to know what is really necessary for our body.

Remember this: your mind subsists wholly, or nearly so, on the body. Your body must furnish the material for your mind to work upon, and every thought that we think is the product of the senses. Consciousness is a sensation; and can we think clearly, logically, and reasonably, if the organs of our body are constantly crying out under the distortion of some abnormal habit? Certainly not. Abnormal habits will produce like mental conditions; and abnormal mental conditions will produce abnormal habits in our body. Thus both must be brought into harmony before the mind can think logically and reasonably. When we can bring our appetites, passions, desires, feelings, and emotions into perfect harmony with pure simple nature, then we are ready to take the second step in the unfoldment of the mental faculties, into the experiment of knowledge of the relation that our mind bears to the universal mind and the mind-governing processes of the solar system, where we shall find prolific fields of research and knowledge. When we have brought our physical senses into perfect harmony with nature then we shall see how distorted are our present methods of life; then everything within us will cry out for pure nature. That will lay the foundation for a reorganization of everything in our present age.

If man and woman at the present time will begin with eating and drinking, and bring their appetites and passions up to pure nature we shall wield a power that will ramify through every department of domestic, social, and religious life, and our government will be made a government for the benefit of all the people, and not a government of oppression and repression of the higher faculties. This will lay the foundation to bring in the Divine order in nature, to bring about the answer to the prayer that the Nazarene taught his people to pray: First the recognition of Our Father, source of our being and author of our existence. "Let Thy kingdom come." Not, "let me die and pass to a better world," but "let Thy kingdom come, and Thy will be done in this world among men, as perfectly as it is now done by the perfected souls who live in the realms of light, in the heavens!" What will that amount to? Think of it. When the dominating will, the mind and purity, and spirituality of the Infinite is obtained upon the earth to that degree that his will has become the will of all living, to that perfect extent that every one of us will obey as implicitly, as perfectly, as the angels of the heaven obey it. Could you conceive of any other heaven? What is heaven? Harmony with the laws of our own being, that is heaven; that will bring happiness, and that is the only method by which happiness can ever be obtained.

Now, suppose a method should be propounded to you whereby you could bring this body into perfect harmony with the laws of its nature; of course, that would produce

THE SUBJUGATION OF THE BODY.

perfect health; perfect health would be perfect happiness, so far as the body is concerned. Bring the mind into perfect harmony with the Mind of the Universe! Then all antagonism, all cause of combat, all difficulties, all oppression and suppression will have passed away. And when that is accomplished, disease will become an impossibility, because all disease arises first in the mind, in the mental conditions, and afterwards reacts and disorders the physical body; thus when we come into harmony with Spirit, which is the God of the universe, sickness, sorrow, pain, and death will disappear.

Death? Yes. Death will pass away with all the other curses. We are taught that death is a necessity, that death is a friend. Yes, death is a friend to some at a very early age. We find persons who, through distortion of all their nature and mentality, have become so oppressed by reacting nature that death to them is more than welcome, and notwithstanding the fears of what may be in the beyond they take their own lives. Then death is only a friend to such as have distorted and debauched their own divine character, until it is unfit for existence any further. The teachings of Christ, and all the masters of antiquity, were not teachings of death, but of life. At this present time there are people known as occultists who claim that there are men now living that have lived for thousands of years. They go when they wish and return when they wish. This may seem strange, but it is a large subject.

When we have brought our minds and appetites into harmony with universal law, so that we can think intelligently and see Mother Nature in all her processes, we shall find that we, each of us, are the epitome of the universe; not only the epitome of the physical universe, but the quintessence of all that there is in the universe, the Spirit of God included;—the recognition of "Our Father" in the Lord's Prayer. God is Spirit. Are you? Question yourself. If you are Spirit what consciousness have you of it. Spirit is inconceivable from the physical sense; you cannot touch, taste, or smell Spirit; it is that intangible something that the gross physical senses can never know. Then, can you believe in the existence of such a thing that is intangible to the five senses? How can you say "Our Father" unless perchance you have made an image of a man, and are recognizing only the physical appearance; if so, then you have broken the first Commandment where it is said: "Thou shall not make unto thee any graven image or any likeness of anything that is in the heaven above or on the earth beneath or in the waters under the earth; thou shalt not bow down thyself to them nor serve them etc." If you recognize as supreme the material body and bow down to that, you are worshiping only flesh which is constantly passing away into vapor and becoming earth.

The Oriental teachers, way back in the mystic past, have all united in its being a necessity that man, in order to make attainments in spiritual unfoldment, should regard the physical body as something impure, unclean, from the fact that it is constantly dissolving, decaying and belongs to the grosser element of a physical world. It is undoubtedly true that every thought found in the Hebrew Bible and Christian Testament is intended to lead away from flesh, to recognize only Spirit as the real, and it will be just to say that all teachers of spiritual science have united in the effort to lead us to think that the body should only be regarded as the animal, which serves the intellectual and spiritual man, and as an animal that does good service, it should be carefully protected and looked after in all that is necessary for it, in order to make it a good and useful creature here. We should not love flesh, nor the things of the flesh, but we should love spirit. We should and must, before we can accomplish anything like these attainments, taught by all the teachers of every bible and every doctrine and by the spiritual and cause-world, first recognise that each individual is Spirit.

So all that pertains to the physical body, to the intellectual and spiritual man, in order to make it what it should be, rests upon the one foundation; harmony with its own nature and with the laws of that nature that projected it into being. When that time shall come, when we can find men and women that will begin to take hold of the first principles, to prepare, develop, unfold and perfect their physical bodies and also their mental faculties, we shall rise like a powerful army of men and women who, having built a foundation of knowledge, understanding and wisdom so far superior to anything that is known in the world to-day, would control the physical forces and govern the nations of the world and by means of this harmony in their own nature, could, at will, turn their attention from this world of phenomena to a world of cause and know with equal accuracy the causes, as well as the effects, and through cause trace out and obtain the knowledge of all that pertains to the uses of this life.

If any person could be brought to believe that there was no hope in ever finding a place of rest, of harmony and happiness, at once there would spring up in that bosom a desire to cease to be. All hope would disappear; there would be nothing to live for. The whole world is living in a vague hope for divine rest and happiness, or heaven, a heaven of their own ideal, let it be what it may. The world has been governed, for ages past, by the animal forces and propensities, and is so to-day. The animal passions, inflamed from the hells beneath, rule humanity. Now, the thing for men and women who have the capacity to think, is to let go of everything that binds them to this age and order of things, to go to work on their own body, on their own mind, on their own powers, and see to it that they come into harmony with the universal law; and when this can be accomplished we shall find ourselves drawn together by a common bond of sympathy, as perfectly as one organ of our body is united to another. We shall find that we are as inseparable, as one organ is from another. When we have come into that harmonious unity, then God's will has become the ruling power of our will, and then his kingdom has come, and his will is done in this body and through this body; and the kingdoms of the world will be saved from destruction; and this alone can save this age and our people from the inevitable consequences of a distorted life. We are not working here merely for self-gratification, but for the good of all men. We are working so that, if possible, we may awaken men and women to the work of harmonizing their own natures, within and with the universal will, so that they may become the saviours of the world. When this body is thus brought together, perfected and *organized*, then will be fulfilled that glorious vision that is given in Revelation XXI. and XXII. chapters. The reason why we have never understood that book was that our minds have been in such chaos that we could not perceive any of the objects and purposes of the Creator. When we can realize the fact that there was a definite object in the mind of the Creator and that it was to make man LIKE HIMSELF, and " let them have dominion over the fish of the sea and fowl of the air and over all the earth," then we shall recognize what ultimate the angel was talking to John about, Rev. VII. chapter, an ultimate wherein a great multitude "of the first fruit of the earth," the pure minds, the perfected souls of men, would be gathered out of every tribe and tongue of the nation, gathered into organic harmony in the world. Then "the kingdoms of THIS WORLD will have become the kingdoms of our Lord and his Christ." Rev. XI. 15.

Q. I would like to ask for a little more light from Prof. Butler. He spoke once before, and he has come to the point again to-day, in regard to God. In one lecture he quoted from Genesis where God created man by the word of his power. That would seem to give us the idea that God created man at a particular day, a particular hour, and it gives us the process of Creation. Then he says man came up from a lower order of being, taking perhaps thousands or millions of years to come up to what he is to-day. There seems to be a contradiction. If it took millions of years how is he going to harmonize these two theories?

Another question concerning God's creating man and, at the same time, the other things: if he regards God as an intellectual being, since he tells us God is in the wind and stone and everywhere, — I want to know: is God simply a force in Nature, or is he an intellectual, active being of intelligence?

A. The last question would necessarily be first; answering the first would answer the second. We believe that God is an infinite being; viz., is all things that are. In all stages of existence elements, principles or qualities, all are part of one infinite whole. God is the great soul of the universe, each world is but a mind-organ of the

Infinite, and the thinking process of the Infinite mind-movement is ever active. Our little planet is the mind-organ that represents the love and sympathy and order of the heart. In company with all the other functions this member of the solar system is constantly in motion around its parent centre, under the control of that centre as the will that governs it; and as each of these worlds moves at different speed, and this movement is but the movement of the brain of the Infinite Mind, these movements like the movements of your brain are forming thoughts and projecting them into the space between these worlds, but which is all interfilled by one dense sea of life. These thought-forms were known in the ages of antiquity, and were called the "aggregers" of worlds and systems which, in turn, react upon these worlds, are drawn in, inspired wherever there are chemical qualities existing, adapted as a receptacle of it; and these chemical qualities are caused to act according to the quality of the thought that is created by the movements of those worlds and drawn into it. Thus, every plant, every animal and every man is a thought-creation of the God of the Universe. And we are not left to a simple belief of it, because we have received from the higher intelligence a knowledge of the law of the universe and have given it to the world in the form of Solar Biology through which anyone can, by knowing the time when the individual came into existence, tell the thoughts that were in the mind-organs of the Creator. Each individual is the expression of a thought in a single form. We have in our own experiences found that when our mind was quickly changed from one method of thought to another, — and we believe others have had similar experiences,—we could feel the convolutions in our brain change position. The process of the brain in thinking is a process of motion and the processes of the motions of the heavenly bodies are the processes of the Mind of God.

Those of you who have read our lecture on the "Idea of God" can see that we convey the idea that God is everything. But, lest we err here, we want to remember that what we call the ether is but the finer essence of life, a quality of thought and conscious existence; and that we can inspire, and form out of this life-essence, thoughts and send them forth just as we are told God did in the beginning,—and they become things. Thus, you see, in this thought we may go on further than our solar system which is the brain organs of the God of this system.

Thoughts are formed in each man, woman, and living thing. We stand now as an ultimate intelligence that is able through the brain-power of the Universe to begin to understand this universal law and the source of being, the God of the Universe, and we find we are not the only individuals, but that there are beings who have passed beyond the confines of a physical life and have come into harmony with the one body of the heavens, as members of that body, which is the God of our system. These grand and perfected souls love our earth, they have thrown off all selfishness, all hate, all passion, and as God is love and as they are the expression of that love, these grand souls love to come and guide and instruct and lead each of us into a realization of that love. They will lead us, illuminate our minds, unfold our inner consciousness, and give us an understanding of all great things and bring us into that Divine harmony that they are in. They as one body and we as one body will unite in order to rule all the affairs of the planet earth through reciprocal action of the God of the system. Thus, you see, we believe in an intelligent, conscious, thinking, active, reasoning God in whose organic and inorganic life are all things that we possess and many millions of other attributes and principles that we cannot yet conceive.

And through conjunction with that Infinite we may unfold without end.

Q. Do you think there are many who can comprehend the Infinite?

A. There is a great difference between comprehending and understanding. We may understand but not comprehend. It is possible to have an understanding of God, and to get the basic principles. When we understand the laws governing this physical body, we will have an understanding of God in his and her relation to us.

Now one more word in regard to the question. If God created the world by a word, it must have been done at a particular time, and time is measured by the movement of worlds. If you give the day of birth of your child we know the exact word he is the expression of, and by knowing what word came into physical structure we know at what time it was spoken. Those who have scientific data (we say scientific, because it proves true always and therefore is a scientific fact), know that the movements of the worlds are the creations of thought. Matter did not have any beginning: Matter and Spirit and God are all the same. Mind had never a beginning, and Mind, God and Spirit are the same in ultimates, but different in conditions, and manifestation. They are constanly changing. Worlds are being born as much as men are being born. There was a word of God, and out of that germinal word of God there will start multifarious thought-forms. Thus God is talking all the time and always will be. **In order that we** may know anything there must be the positive and negative, light and dark, cold and heat.

In the beginning, when man was down upon a low plane, he acted out his brute nature and it was necessary that he should learn lesson after lesson, and by virtue of those experiments we have power to think. Otherwise we would be like brutes. They know they live. They act under the impulse of the universal mind, but have no power of reasoning. This is the one condition which has helped to develop you and me. Therefore whilst there was a time when Mercury, Venus, Earth, Mars, etc., were born, yet there is no time taking the aggregate of the First Cause; eternity is the same yesterday, to-day and forever; only matter is constantly changing, thoughts are being formed and so God is constantly renewing himself from the worlds he has made, and again aggregating worlds of the lower elements that are no longer useful in the higher sphere. When you understand the workings of your own bodies you can understand the workings of the Infinite.

We fitly conclude this lecture with another selection from the *Lyric of the Golden Age.*

> Rapid as light flashed from the scimetar
> Of Dawn, who rides triumphant in his car,
> Sun-axled, through the city of the stars,
> Came to king Alfred a white messenger,
> And the pale dreamer, lifted up, was led
> Into that Heaven whence man below is fed
> With power and beauty. 'Tis the sanctuary
> Of the Creative Spirit, who doth fill
> The universe. As clouds that brightening vary
> From gray to crimson o'er some eastern hill.

The poet's mind grew bright. This vision there
He saw forth-mirrored in supernal air.
In his own speech, as afterward he told
The vision, let the mystic scene unfold.

 I saw in Heaven an orbed, revolving brain
Teeming with thoughts. "This," said my guide to me,
"Is Nature, whose vast macrocosmic fane
Is the creative shrine of Deity.
Through the great cosmic brain eternally
Worlds are led forth to run their brightening race,
And heavens unfold their white immensity
In its dominions, and material space
This orb's descending sphere doth compass and embrace.

 The sun of suns, wherefrom all systems flow,
As thoughts from their deep fountain, thou shalt see."
As thus he spake there came a sudden glow
Of inspiration; then it seemed to me
That I became a wondrous trinity,
A threefold being; thought and will and feeling
Within me grew distinct; I woke to be
Triune, and slowly through my nature stealing,
There came a voice, this mighty truth revealing.

 "Nature is an impersonal trinity,
And altogether in the form of man,
Cause, Means and End in threefold unity
Exist, and shape Creation's wondrous plan.
God is the Cause; in Him all things began.
That Cause is Love, Essence and Effluence,
Wisdom and Means, whereby with three-fold span
All things are fashioned. Love and Wisdom blend,
As cause and means; from their full unity descend

 Inspiring operation; these are seven
From three and three from one, supreme, divine.

These formed the sun of suns, the heaven of heaven
To be the matrix of all forms; and time
Began when that great orb began to shine,
And space, which lives in its proceeding sphere.
The macrocosm is a perfect trine,
Threefold in heat, light, substance, atmosphere,
And all in all, through all, God doth to all appear.

Whatever is, was and shall be forever.
All forms are in their atoms destined to
Unfold new atoms from within, whenever
Divine proceeding forces shape a new
Germ form within; wherever three or two
Atoms are found, God in the midst is there;
Atoms, no less than spirits, in his view
Are precious, and he maketh each his care;
Each atom hath its form, stamped with God's impress fair.

Atoms are trinities, no less than men;
Ones, threes, and sevens, celestial spiralines,
Or globes or curves. God gives to each of them
A separate use; globe-atoms heat sublimes
And they grow ripe. Each opens its pure shrines,
Gives birth to curves, and these in their connection
Expand, and, from their most interior climes,
The spiral atoms rise in sweet perfection;
These are the germs of men; each hath its own affection.

Mind-atoms are all spiralines. The brain
Grows from their aggregation corporate.
Mind-atoms, once conjoined, no stress of pain
From their affinities can segregate,
Being homogeneous, each hath a gate
That opens immostly to God Most High;
These atoms coalesce, amalgamate
In essence, and co-operate in three
Discrete degrees, and these compose Humanity.

The seminal glands discrete and separate
The different ranks of atoms, and attract
The spiralines; they blend in perfect state.
When the maternal ovaries co-act
A spiral vortex then is formed, in fact
The embryo of man. It hath its shape
From the creative energy; compact,
Indissolubly wed, its atoms take
The human form and drink in love and truth, — and wake.

The primates of all substance are divided
In three degrees. The spiralines form souls.
Th' harmonic waves of ether, many-tided,
Whereof to every orb a volume rolls,
Are freighted with their virtue; from the poles
Evenly spread, o'er sea and land diffused
Through all the pores of earth; and God controls
Their spiral movement; they are interfused
Through air and sea and land, and through all minds transfused.

This is the end of this publication.

Any remaining blank pages are for our book binding requirements and are blank on purpose.

To search thousands of interesting publications like this one, please remember to visit our website at:

http://www.kessinger.net